What We Learned from Uncle Lester

Volume 1

Bill Goins and Tony Hancock

Parson's Porch Books

What We Learned from Uncle Lester
ISBN: Softcover 978-1-955581-95-0
Copyright © 2024 by Bill Goins and Tony Hancock

Parson's Porch Books is an imprint of Parson's Porch & Company (PP&C) in Cleveland, Tennessee. PP&C is a self-funded charity which earns money by publishing books of noted authors, representing all genres. Its face and voice is **David Russell Tullock** (dtullock@parsonsporch.com).

Parson's Porch & Company *turns books into bread & milk* by sharing its profits with the poor.

www.parsonsporch.com

What We Learned from Uncle Lester

Contents

Chapter 1

Why We Wrote This Book

God does not call the equipped, God equips the called

This book, *What We Learned from Uncle Lester*, Volume 1 has been written for our grandkids, (Quin, Delmont, Lillie, Lukas, Hudson, Hadley, and Lauren), our great grandkids, and their kids, and their kids, etc., and for anyone who may someday be called to the ministry. We have written this book for you, young pastor (full or part time), for all music ministers that may be thrust into the pulpit because there is no one else available to steer the ship, and for all Chaplains. We did not write it to get rich, or famous. If you own more than 50 acres, you are rich.

If you have ever written a book, you are famous. We are all rich and famous through God's grace. We wrote this book because everyone, especially our grandkids, deserves to know the truth about the past. The American Civil war was not fought over slavery, global warming, and the critical race theory are both lies, and the great reset must be stopped. And if we have any foresight about the future, and we do, we need to share that with you now. As we wrote this book, we often felt like the Old Testament prophet, Amos, writing to the nation of Israel. Our message is the same as his. Our nation, America must repent and change our ways, or our country will all surely die. Our country is almost spiritually dead. Communism using socialism, liberalism, and progressivism has established control over many of our social spheres, politics, economics, laws, education, media, art, and culture5. Joe Bidens recent executive order funding biotechnology and biomanufacturing will lay the way for a Satanic Utopia. This is really scarry. The Bible must be placed back in our public schools and our kids taught to read it and love it. The bible has been removed from many schools, but in Hamilton County Tennessee, the bible has been taught for 100 years. Actually, you can earn 3 hours college credits at Chattanooga State for the Old Testament history class you can take in the Hamilton County Bibles in the School Program. This program does not cost the taxpayers anything.

Amos wrote about 42 years before God allowed Israel (the Northern Kingdom) to be captured by Assyria, and about 179 years before Judah (the Southern Kingdom) was captured by Babylon. How long will it be before God allows America to fall to the Chinese and Russians? We believe, it won't be long. Major changes are needed in our government and especially in our public education system so students will once again learn to love God, read the bible, work hard and not be dependent on the government.

This is very important. Grandkids get this if you don't get anything else from this book. There are two voices talking to you constantly. The good voice, which is the Holy Spirit, the bad voice, which is the devil, or satin. Sometimes these two voices will both sound good. The way you tell the difference is simple. If what you are hearing or being told conflicts with scripture, it is the voice of the devil. The only way you can distinguish which voice is true, is by constantly reading and studying your bible. The more you read, the more you study, the easier it is to determine which is the good voice. For example, many say that a woman has the right to do whatever she wants with her body. But the bible says that abortion is murder. So which voice do you listen too? The voice that agrees with scripture. It's very simple. Don't murder. But if you never read the bible because it has been taken out of your schools, and your parents did not drag you to Sunday school and VBS like ours did, you will never know which voice is right and which one is wrong. This is not hard to understand. If you are a pastor, people will ask you which is the good voice. Don't just tell them what you think they want to hear. Many pastors do that to maintain harmony in the flock. Some denominations have even ordained homosexual pastors. How dumb. If you find yourself in one of those unbiblical churches leave quietly today.

The authors, Bill Goins and Tony Hancock, are first cousins, Southern Baptist and retired engineers. We both studied engineering at the University of Tennessee. But before we went to college, we learned a few things from our Uncle Lester. So, what did we learn? Love God, pray, save your money, work hard, read the Bible, buy land because the communists someday will try to take away your land), always pay your bills on time, no student loans and no credit card debt, always tell the truth, don't gamble, don't bet on racehorses, take your kids fishing (remember most of Jesus's disciples were fishermen and he is a storyteller), teach your grandkids stories, teach them how to shoot a gun, paddle a canoe, spend quality time outdoors, crawl through caves, send them to bible school summer camp, and teach them to always do the right thing even when no one's watching. Because God is always watching. While you are sitting in the boat fishing, tell them the story of Jonah and the whale. God sent Jonah to Nineveh, the capital of Assyria, the same country that would someday capture Israel. The Ninevites quickly forgot everything that God taught them through Jonah.

Every chance you get, buy land because someday your government may try to take away your land[2]. The communists will try to take away your land.

9

This book is titled *What We Learned from Uncle Lester, Volume 1.* It's our prayer that you too have an Uncle Lester in your life who will teach you how to love God, pray, study your Sunday School lesson reach week, fish, hunt, shoot straight, work hard, tell stories. Some of the stories you tell your grand kids may actually be true. If you don't have an Uncle Lester in your life to tell you stories, maybe you can be an Uncle Lester to someone who needs a little help. God's work, ministry, is Hard Work and Hard Work is best learned while you are young. Programs like Boy Scouts (before they went liberal), Trail Life USA, American Heritage Girls, Taekwondo, 4- H, Royal Ambassadors, school sports, band, etc., are essential for building good work habits while you are young. And when your kids are old enough and can shoot straight, help them join the NRA and get them a carry permit. They must be 21 to buy their own handgun in Tennessee. You cannot give them a handgun.

You will not get rich in ministry, by earthly monetary standards, but you will be laying up treasures in Heaven. And it's hard work. To our grandkids, great grandkids and their kids and their kids ......, who may be called to the ministry, engineering is a lot easier. We know. We have both been there. Study engineering like your uncle Will, or study to become a veterinarian like Karen, or a dentist like Uncle Clay or an architect like Uncle Steve or any medical field. But to be like Uncle Clay it takes 10 hard years of college. We pray that you will learn now to work hard at whatever you do, and love God.

The Epoch Times[1] reported on Aug 3-9, 2022, that Argentina's Government is rapidly collapsing because of out-of-control spending. Are our government programs causing this same problem? The answer is yes. Just last week our government announced that they would wave payments for student loans. The mainstream media went wild. It means that those of us that did not go to college, who worked and saved, will pay off the loans of others. Does that sound fair to you? But college student loan forgiveness was such a bad idea that a few weeks after the announcement, the government changed its mind and announced that most college loans would not all be forgiven. Our great news media scarcely mentioned this correction. But they had big headlines when the loan forgiveness idea was first announced. How is that for reporting the news? America is on a collision course to total disaster because of our out-of-control government's spending. Just like Argentina. Have you ever noticed how social security increases, stimulus checks and student loan wavers are always announced just before a national election? Our country is following the same path that Israel traveled after King Solomon's death (2 Kings). And We predict that God will allow Russia and China to destroy America just like he allowed Babylon and Assyria to destroy the divided nation of Israel. Nothing happens unless God's hand is on it. Pastors, you should be aware of where our country is headed. Read the book of Amos, which was written just 30 years before Israel (the Northern Kingdom) was captured by Assyria. Then Judah (the Southern Kingdom) was captured by Babylon. God may allow this to happen to America someday[5]. Probably not in our lifetime but likely during yours.

Another example of the rapid decay in America is a recent action by Alaska Airline, which sent an e-mail to all employees urging them to support current legislation relative to LBGT rights. The e-mail asks the employs to respond if they had an opinion on the subject. Two flight attendants replied that they were offended by the company's position. So, what did Alaska Air do? They fired the two flight attendants. When companies conduct open discrimination against employees, communism is not far away. Will Alaska Airline get away with it? It depends on who the judge is. We are losing our freedom of religion.

So, what's a couple of concerned Baptists supposed to do? Write a book. This book. You need to read it if you are kin to us or new to the ministry or if you are a chaplain. If you are a music minister who has been thrusted into the pulpit, there are some things here that you need to know.

Who did we write this book for? The reporters and editors of the *Epoch Times* don't need this book. They know what's happening in America. Kent Evens and his friends at Trail Life USA don't need this book because they see the light. Our political leaders know what's happening. But they love it this way. They are getting rich. They are the problem. Mark Smith CEO of the 100-year-old firearms manufacturer, Smith & Wesson, was asked to testify before a congressional committee.

Read his reply at:
https://www.smithwesson.com/sites/default/files/press-release/Smith%20%26%20Wesson%20CEO%20Issues%20Strong%20Statement%20in%20the%20Face%20of%202nd%20Amendment%20Attacks_8_15_Final.pdf.

Global warming is a hoax, a malicious deception. Probably the biggest worldwide lie in the last 100 years. We have devoted an entire chapter to the lie, global warming.

Young pastors fresh out of seminary and you never-been-to seminary pastors taking extension classes from Samford University, Ministerial Training Institute, you need this book. Transitional Interim pastors trying to salvage a broken congregation following a disastrous church split, need a little guidance and lots of prayer. Also, Chaplains of all denominations will find some useful encouragement between these pages. So, read on. You should know by now whether or not you want to buy this book. And you should know whether or not you are going to read it. Don't buy this book to give to another pastor. He already has too many books. Actually, He and you only need one book, the Bible. Because history repeats itself. Everything that's happening now has been predicted in the Bible. Just as God allowed the Assyrians and then the Babylonians to capture his chosen people, God will surely allow America to fall to the Chinese and the Russians. The fall is underway. The freedom wall is falling. Our freedoms are being taken away every day. Electric cars are not needed. Electric cars are a bad idea. Don't ever buy one. The Utilities will have to spend $trillions to enlarge the national electric power grid to support the proposed renewable energy demands4. Many nuclear power plants have been cancelled, that would have provided the needed electric power to support electric cars. Hurricane Lin that passed through Florida dumped salt water on new electric cars. Some of those cars caught on fire. Lithium batteries and salt water do not mix well. Electric car owners in Florida have been told to not park there can inside the garage. Take it from a couple of engineers, gas- and diesel-powered vehicles are the best way to ride to work and to church.

Any business owner in America will tell you that he cannot find enough workers. People will work for a couple of days and then tell the employer that "this is not for me, I quit". Where did they learn that? We believe that our public school system has totally failed them. When you are in the second grade and you don't finish your homework, your teacher will just say "that's OK sweetie, I love you, and you don't have to do this work." After 12 years of not having to do any work, kids learn that the world does not expect them to do any work and they will not do any. Single parent homes don't help. What does the Bible say about work? The Manufacturing Institute3 predicts that by 2030, the manufacturing sector will have 2.1 million unfilled positions, which will cost the US an estimated $1 trillion in GDP.

Read Mark Smith's letter to congress. It's not the school's fault. Our out-of-control government spending and liberal policies established by the liberals is the problem. Later in this book you will learn why you should never vote for a liberal. Uncle Lester taught Sunday school every Sunday for over 40 years. He never voted for a liberal.

The chapters in this book are in general arranged in chronological order. The oldest stories are listed first and the latest stories last. You should know by now that the books in the Bible are not arranged chronologically. Except in F. LaGard Smiths' "The Narrated Bible". Which we recommend for your annual bible reading plan. You goal should be to read through the entire bible each year. By the fourth year you will start to understand it.

Our government just announced that Social Security benefits will increase by 8.7 % this year. This is the largest increase in benefits in 40 years Why was this announced just a few weeks before a national election? Last month it was announced that student loans would be forgiver. But just a few weeks later, our government announced that they had changed their mind and many loans would not be forgiven. Strange things get announced just before a national election.

The Epoch Times1 just reported that the Communists Chinese CCC just opened a POLICE STATION in New York City. While we agree that the NYPD can certainly use some help, why does the CCC need a police station anywhere in America? This is part of the CCC's worldwide effort to control the world. What rights does a New Yorker have if arrested by the CCC police force? China has 54 police service centers opened by the

Chinese authorities outside of mainland China. They are reportedly used for coercion to repatriate Chinese people and might be a tool for sabotage or espionage6.

It has also been reported1 that our state department has just told all American tourists to get out of Russia. A Pfizer Exec just admitted that the COVID-19 Vaccine Was Not Tested on Preventing Transmission Before Release. The end may be closer than we think[5]. Read fast.

2 Thessalonians 3:10

"For even when we were with you, we gave you this rule: The one who is unwilling to work shall not eat."

Chapter 2

Our Grandpa Will Goins

Our Grandpa was the hardest working person we ever knew. William Doris Goins was the original SAGE CON. Which is defined as a Spiritually Active Governance Engaged Conservative. He was born in 1875. Ten years after the end of the Civil War. He raised 9 kids on a small farm, where they grew everything they ate. He built his own house, his barn and his blacksmith shop from the lumber he cut on his farm with his own sawmill. He was constantly repairing things at his church. Grandpa never owned a car or tractor. He farmed with two mules. He read the bible every day and He never failed to vote in an election.

I remember his house before it had TVA electricity. Grandpa had lights. Grandpa's original lights were powered by a gas generator he had installed in the garage. When it was starting to get dark, Grandma would say "Will, it's time to crank the generator." He would not move. He was talking to us grandkids. Grandpa was a great storyteller. So, a little later she would come back and say, "Will, I said it's time to crank the generator!". So, then he would go out to the garage, pour a little gas in the generator and give it a crank. He would let us grandkids try to crank it, but we were not strong enough. But when he pulled the rope, instantly lights came on in the house. How long the lights were on depended on how much fuel he put in the tank. We all knew that when the gas ran out, the lights would flicker and almost go out. Then the lights would come on for about 20 seconds. After that it was dark. We knew that when the lights flickered, we had about 20 seconds to be under the covers. The lights would not come back on that night.

I heard Grampa tell the ice man "Joe I am going to try out this new TVA electricity stuff. I am tired of cranking that generator every night. The new electric refrigerator will set right here on the front porch next to your old Ice Box. If you ever come by here and that refrigerator is gone, leave me a block of Ice." Joe drove a one-horse wagon to deliver the ice.

We got a new preacher at the church and Grandma invited the new preacher and his wife to come home with us for Sunday dinner. It was this preacher first Sunday. Not many preachers get invited to people's homes for dinner anymore. Him and his wife came, and it was a special lunch. Lots of fine food. We had just sat down when there was a knock on the back-screen door. Our neighbor Jed Galtian was standing at the door. His mule was tied on the porch. He said "Will, my mule has just thrown a shoe. Can you fix him for me? I got to get that back field plowed before it rains tomorrow night. "

Grandpa did not say anything, he just got up, pushed back his plate and went to change clothes. I went with him. But I did not change clothes. One hour later Jed's mule had a new iron shoe. I heard Jeb say "Will, what do I owe you? "Grandpa just said "Nothing Jed, just bring me some corn when your crop comes in." After Jed left, I ask Grandpa, "why did you not charge him something?" Grandpa said "Jed does not have any money, Whatever I ask him for, He could not pay. And he would be embarrassed because he did not have any money. So, it's best just to fix the mule so they can work. He would do the same thing for me" What I learned was that it is better to fix a problem, so work can be done, than to collect a little money.

When we got back in the house, the preacher and his wife were gone and lots of the food was gone, but we still got one slice of fresh apple pie. Grandma was a little upset because the preacher's wife did not offer to stay and help her clean up the kitchen. When you cook on a wood stove, it can take as long to clean up as it did to cook the meal. This preacher's wife did not know about helping in the kitchen. We assumed that her family must have had a maid. Grandpa taught all his kids how to work hard. He taught Uncle Lester. Grandpa never failed to vote in an election. He told us about the Civil war. It was not about slavery.

Chapter 3

The Best Chevrolet Truck Salesman in Tennessee

Our Uncle Lester's brother Lloyd Goins was recognized by Chevrolet Motor Company as the best Chevrolet Truck Salesman in Tennessee. I saw the certificate. Here's how he did it. On his small desk, he had 3 roto desks of phone numbers. On the first he had the name and phone number of everyone in Bradley county that could afford a new Chevrolet Pick Up Truck. In the second roto desk he had the names and phone numbers of everyone in Bradley County that could only afford a used Chevrolet Truck. On the third roto desk he had the phone numbers, if they had a phone, of all the poor people in Bradley county that really could not afford any vehicle. But he had helped them get a truck before and they needed it on the farm. When Bradley Motor Company got in a shipment of new trucks, he would start calling those on disk one and the conversation would go something like this. "How are you doing? How is your family doing? How many miles do you have on that truck I sold you last year? That Truck still running well? We just got in a new shipment of new trucks. You may want to come by next week and test drive one of them. The new models have many new features that you would like. I will see you next Tuesday.

After he sold that new truck and got the trade in, He would call those on the second roto disk and the conversation would go something like this "How are you doing? How is your family doing? How many miles do you have on that truck I sold you last year? That Truck still running well? We just got a trade in that you may be interested in. You may want to come by next week and test drive this one. It has many features that your old truck does not have. I can make you a good deal on this trade in. This truck may need a set of tires, but we can help you with that. Great, I will see you next Wednesday."

When he got the second truck in, and a used set of tires, He would call those on the third roto disk. And the conversation would go something like this "How are you doing? How is your family doing? How many miles do you have on that truck I sold you last year? That Truck still running well? I know you can't afford to trade trucks, but we just got a good truck in that you may be interested in. You may want to come by next week and test drive this one. It may need different tires, but we just got some good used tires we can put on it for you at no cost. It has many new features that you would like. I will see you next Friday and I will help you get it financed."

Lloyd would sell the same truck 3 times. New, once used and twice used. To Chevrolet Motors he had sold 3 trucks. He could have made more money selling only new trucks but that was not his goal. His goal was to help everyone get good transportation. Lloyd was the choir director at the Church of God. All the men in his Choir and the Preacher drove Chevrolet trucks. You could not take him fishing because he would say "Hay, paddle the boat over there, I need to talk to that man about a truck." His mission field was good trucks for everyone.

Chapter 4

Ressie Goins

Ressie Goins, Tony's mother, was a natural athlete. She could play any sport, but basketball seemed to be her sweet spot. The basketball coach at the Charleston High School noticed her and wanted her to play for his team. But there was no way for her to get from east Bradley County to the Charleston High School each day. So, the basketball coach bought a car and talked her older brother Lester in to driving her to school each day. Lester was the oldest of 9 kids and had dropped out of High School to help on the farm. At that time, it was not uncommon for the oldest son to stay home and work on the farm. Well after Lester drove Ressie to school each day there was nothing for him to do except go to school. So, the principal re-admitted him and he eventually graduated. Even though he was too old to legally attend a Tennessee High School.

After Ressie finished her very successful basketball career at Charleston HS she was offered several college scholarships but turned them down to marry Harry Hancock. She worked so he could go to college. Student Loads had not been invented. Thus, they had no student loans.

Lester bought an old school bus that he drove for several years. Then he used that old bus as a down payment on a filling station which he ran for several years. Then He sold this filling station to buy his first farm.

His farm was a dairy farm, with lots of quality Jersey cows. And a few bulls. But he did not milk these cows. He hired a tenant family, the Gates, to milk the cows every day. He provided them with a house to live in. Cows have to be milked every day. Lester also owned two milk trucks. The trucks took raw milk to the creamery each day. But he did not drive these trucks.

He hired two drivers to drive to several dairy farms, pick up the fresh milk in large 10-gallon cans and deliver it to the creamery each day. He charged each farmer a hauling fee based on how much milk the farmer shipped to the creamery.

He also had a ½ acre tobacco allotment. You can grow a lot of tobacco on ½ acre. He worked the tobacco with the Gates family on the halves. Which meant Lester bought all the tobacco seeds, the fertilizer, arsenic (to kill the tobacco worms), and provided the building to store the tobacco until it was dry enough to take to the tobacco sales barn. After the tobacco was sold, he gave one half of the sales check to the Gates Family. They got exactly half. The check was usually several thousand dollars. And the tobacco was usually sold just before Christmas. As other adjacent farms became for sale, he would buy them. Eventually owning several hundred acres. Not bad for a guy who dropped out of High School. All his farm hands and truck drivers were treated fairly and always given a fair wage. And they worked for him for several years. Bottom line: Treat people fairly and they will stay with you. Sounds like Sam Walton of Wal-Mart. It's the same principle. If you work hard, save your money, treat people fairly, you too can own a 100-acre farm. Tony and Bill both own farmland. We learned that from Uncle Lester. He learned it from his father, our grandfather Will Goins. Ressie learned hard work from her daddy Will Goins.

Proverbs 13:22 says, "A good person leaves an inheritance for their children's children,"

That's our grandchildren, We should leave our grandchildren land.

Chapter 5

How Tony Hancock Became Pastor of the Hillcrest Baptist Church

Well, the short story is that HCBC offered him exactly the salary that the church could afford and that he could accept. Nothing. Actually, HCBC had been on a downhill spiral for several years. The facility was located in a part of Lexington Ky that was not growing. The deacons and church leaders had actually voted to close the doors. But one member insisted that they try just one more pastor, if they could find one that they could afford? God provided who they needed.

Dr. Tony Hancock had been working as the director of Research for Remington Arms RA following the purchase of RA by IBM. Some argue that IBM did not understand what RA manufactured when they bought the company. The purchase was based on a business evaluation of the profits earned by the company over several years. Once IBM senior management figured out what the company made, they quickly sold it. Mean time Tony Hancock had been sent to RA as Director of Research. The new owners wanted to put their own man in as Director of Research. So, Tony received a rather healthy retirement package, way before he had planned to retire. A perfect match between HCBC need, and Tony's availability to serve without a salary. God does not call the equipped, God equips the called. Having never been to seminary, did not faze the HCBC members. Actually, they liked having a PhD in the pulpit. The church is growing, and they later paid him a salary. This year (2023) Tony retired after 25 years leading HCBC.

Chapter 6

Who Taught Daffy to Fly?

Can American ever fly again?

When Will Goins (IV) and Clay Goins were growing up in Southeast Tennessee, they were surrounded by goats, chickens, pigs, and a pony named Patches. When I, William (III), was growing up, Uncle Lester bought me a pony named Dynamite. One day while I, William Goins (III) was burning brush at the lake, I found a nest containing 3 eggs. Assuming that this was a duck's nest, which it was, and that the mother duck would not come back because of my burning, the three eggs were placed in an incubator already containing Arcana eggs. An Arcana is a South American breed of chicken that lays colored eggs. The next day, 1 of the 3 duck eggs hatched. Will named this duck Daffy. She grew up with a bunch of chickens and for the first part of her life thought that she was a chicken. She would have spent her entire life thinking she was a chicken except for some needed intervention.

A young duck will pattern after whoever is in the pen with her. People do the same thing. God programed Daffy to be a duck, but her family of origin was programming her to be a chicken. When Daffy was about 6 weeks old, we decided that it was time for her to quit being a chicken. Our first attempt to rescue Daffy from a chicken's life was a total failure. The intention was good, but our method was flawed. Chickens don't swim. But ducks are natural swimmers. So, we took Daffy to the lake and thew her in. She immediately ran across the water and raced back to her friends in the chicken pen. We did this several times that day, but Daffy had no interest in water. We could not teach Daffy to swim.

The chickens that Daffy grew up with could not fly because I had clipped one of their wings. Always the right wing. When they tried to fly, they just flopped over because one wing was shorter than the other. That kept the chickens in the uncovered chicken pen.

Several days later Will (IV) had a friend, Mitchell, over for a visit. They decided that even though our family effort to teach Daffy to swim was a disaster, they would try to teach Daffy to fly. The plan was to throw her off the porch. So, they caught Daffy in the chicken pen and threw her off the porch. After an initial hard landing, Daffy realized that she could fly. But she flew back into the chicken pen. The next day Daffy was gone, because Will and Mitchell had taught her how to fly.

We didn't see Daffy for about a year. Then one day after the mulberries were ripe, I saw Daffy walking up the path from the lake to the mulberry tree. This was a new Daffy who was no longer a chicken but was now fully duck.

The next year when the mulberries were ripe, I saw Daffy walking up the path again from the lake to the mulberry tree. Ducks have a fondness for mulberries. But this year she had two ducks following her. She was teaching them to eat mulberries like a duck. We never saw Daffy or her friends at the mulberry tree again.

So, what's the takeaway for this story? If you grow up in a chicken pen although God programed you to be a duck, without someone throwing you off the porch, you will forever be a chicken. Your family of origin can either equip you to fly or keep you on the ground in the chicken pen. Considering the options, you make the choice.

If your parents were on welfare, you will likely be on welfare. If your grandpa was in a union, you will likely be in the same union. You may even become disinclined to work as so many Americans are becoming today. The government will feed you, but you are going to eat stale bread. And eventually, like any good communist, you will learn to like stale bread. But God did not program you to eat stale bread. So, what can you do about it? Answer, work hard, Go to school. Study something that will generate sound income. Not history, K-12 education or political science. Don't get student loans and don't rack up credit card debt. A family on welfare is like a duck in a chicken pin. Education and hard work are the paths out of poverty. Don't take the handouts. You can fly.

The August 3-9, 2022, edition of *The Epoch Times* ran a story by Autumn Stresemann on "Argentina's Collapsing Government. It quotes taxi driver Alvaro Gomez told as saying "I've seen five presidents come and go in that time (15 years); nothing has improved. Half of our country doesn't want a job, and the ones that do, don't want to pay the taxes for the others."

It appears that Argentina's social programs have caused the people to be disinclined to work - ducks that keep on acting like chickens. This is happening in America. Chick-fil-a will hire a new employ, train them for 3 days, and then the new employ comes in and says, "this is not for me, I quit!"

Why does every fast-food restaurant have a sign out front seeking workers? People will not work. I blame the homes and the public schools. If you are in the second grade and you don't do your homework, your teacher will just say, "That's OK sweetheart, I love you, you don't have to do homework." The teachers' unions are killing our kids. Public school teachers don't teach arithmetic, spelling and science anymore. They teach diversity, black lives matter, defunding the police. Why won't people work? They have learned in public school that they don't have to work.

We are rapidly following Argentina's socialistic programs. There are three recent events that clearly show where our country is headed. One is the announcement that a new round of stimulus checks will be sent out just before the November 2022 national elections. All news media (even the woke liberal ones that never say anything bad about a Liberal and have covered up Hunter Biden's corrupt business crimes) have predicted that Liberals will do poorly in the next election. So, what would a pack of evil, power-hungry crooks do? Send everyone a stimulus check to buy your vote and increase social security checks! Have you noticed that stimulus checks always come out just before an election? They are nothing but bribes.

Another clear sign of our march to socialism is the passage of the Inflation Reduction Act (IRA) which authorized 124 billion dollars for the IRS to hire thousands of additional tax auditors to separate the working class from our hard-earned money. This act authorizes 369 billion dollars for energy security and climate change. Actually, climate change is a hoax, and nothing should be spent on this lie. Several years ago, Clint Cooper, Editor of the Chattanooga Times Free-Press clearly documented that Climate Change is a hoax. This funding is intended to fatten the pockets of certain companies. The idiots leading congress are totally out of control. Any representative or senator who voted for this act should be impeached.

A third example is the fight between liberal Congressional Representatives and the Smith and Wesson Company, one of several manufacturers of the popular AR-15 rifle. Mark Smith, CEO of S&W refused to appear for a congressional hearing and submitted the letter referenced in chapter 1. It is clear from his letter that these politicians had nothing beneficial in mind.

S&W is moving their manufacturing facilities from New England to Maryville Tennessee.

Without a vision, the people perish. Recognize your situation and change paths.

Now you know who taught Daffy to fly and you know what the results were, but you don't know who will lead America away from a certain sociological disaster as more people become disinclined to work! Maybe that's you pastor.

What does the New Testament say about those disinclined to work?

2 Thessalonians 3:10

"For even when we were with you, we gave you this rule: "The one who is unwilling to work shall not eat."

But if no one throws the duck off the porch, she will always think she is a chicken. Chickens don't work.

Chapter 7

Who Taught Me to Fly?

You read in the last chapter how my son Will and his friend Mitchel taught our mallard duck Daffy to fly. If you skipped that chapter, go back and read it because it will make this chapter easier to understand. New pastors you are all like Daffy in that your family of origin either propels you forward or holds you back.

The Baptist church I grew up in was very small. One small room where the women met. One larger room where the preaching happened, and the men had Sunday school. And one small room where all us children were corralled, entertained, fed and taught. No indoor plumbing. An outhouse sat just outside the back door of the children's room.

By definition, you were a child until you were baptized. The Sunday after I were baptized, I was promoted from the children's room to the sanctuary. I was saved during a revival in the spring. Baptism was in the Lead Mine Valley creek, a spring fed creek across the gravel road from the church and half-way across a cow pasture. The temperature of a spring fed creeks is about 54oF year-round. Now that's cold. When you have been baptized in a spring fed creek, you remember it.

The next Sunday, I was unceremoniously promoted to the adult class. As soon as I sat down, someone handed me my first Sunday School quarterly, and I was told that a new series of lessons was starting the next week on the Book of Job - and I was teaching it. Well, I still love the Book of Job. I studied every night. By the next Sunday, I was ready to slay them with my great knowledge of Job's journey. I said about 3 sentences and then they taught me. That pattern repeated every Sunday until the quarterly took up a different subject. Those old men taught me to love the Bible and love discussions about the Bible - just like Will and Mitchel taught Daffy to fly by throwing her off the porch. They taught me to study the Bible by throwing me a Sunday School quarterly. They taught me to fly. But Uncle Lester had already taught me Hard Work.

So, 60 years later, what does my resume look like? All because a group of old Baptist men taught me to fly when I was young. This year I was listed in Marquis Who's Who in America 2021.

But in reality, I should have died before I was born. Here's the story. When I was still in my mother's belly, a house fire killed my father and almost killed my mother. During WW2, 1943, gas was rationed. It was easy to get gas and kerosene mixed up. Most people in southeast Tennessee heated with a wood stove. Kerosene was usually used to start the fire in the wood stove. When my father started the fire with what he thought was kerosene, it was actually gasoline and the stove exploded. Setting the house on fire. He got my mother up. Then he exited the building and went around to the other side of the duplex to wake up the family living over there. They got out. But my mother did not get out. She actually fainted inside the burning house. So, after the fire was raging, he went back inside the burning house and carried her out and me to because I was in her belly. He died and she almost died. I lived.

So, what's a widowed mother with a newborn to do? Go on welfare? No way, she got a job with the phone company where she worked for 30 years. We both could have died in that house fire except that my earthly father gave his life to save me. Does this sound at all like how my spherical Father, JESUS, gave his life to save me and you. If you don't know that story, call someone right now.

That's my story. If you have a story, send it to us and we may put it in volume two of this book.

Chapter 8

Red Smith

When I worked as a welding engineering supervisor at Combustion Engineering in Chattanooga, this company was one of the largest employers in town. With over three thousand employees, 300 welders and about 20 welding engineers this company was the largest consumer of welding materials in the country, outside of some large shipyards. The company had grown from the local Welch and Wagner Boiler Company, one of several boiler companies originally in Chattanooga. Today there are no boiler companies in Chattanooga and few in the country, since our government has declared war on fossil power under the hoke global warming stupidity. Move to France if you want reliable electricity.

The mission of our Welding Engineering Department was to:

1. Train the welders

2. Qualify the fabrication procedures

3. Support the shops (surveillance)

Policing the shop floor was the job of the six welding surveillance engineers. Their territory was about 40 acers under roof. A Hugh area and their phones rang constantly.

The best surveillance engineer was a guy named Red Smith. He knew all 300 welders and all of the shop foremen, and He keep up with their families. Because Red was not primarily a welding engineer, he was first of all a Baptist preacher, with a small church in North Georgia. The Combustion Engineering shop floor was his mission field. All 40 acers under roof. When he went out into the shop, he took a copy of the AWS Welding Handbook and a New Testament. But He did not use the welding handbook very much.

I got a call one day from a young very irate shop foreman. It was not unusual to get calls from upset foremen, which happened all day and their current problem was always a crisis that had to be solved right then. Even though the problem may have been around for weeks. This was a new foreman, who told me that he was not getting any work done because Red had all his hand welders huddled up in a prayer meeting. I slipped out into the shop and quickly spotted a group of about 6 workers gathered around Red Smith. I approached the group quietly from behind and discovered that the subject of discussion was the Book of Job. Not a bad subject to discuss with a crew of welders. Welders need all the understanding that they can get. I cut up the steps to the shop office and found the young foreman at his desk working the crossword puzzle in the daily newspaper. I told him that Red was about finished with the group meeting. I ask him, where do you worship? He said he had not been in church for several years but needed to get back in church because his kids were getting older, and they needed it. So, I ask him, the next time you see Red with a group of workers just slip up close enough to hear what is being said and lessen to the discussion. He said he would, and he did. About two weeks later I learned that this foreman and his family had joined a local Church. He never called me again to complain about Red's discussions and I never said anything to Red.

Only God knows the impact of discussions on the shop floor by people like Red Smith. Sometimes it's just a kind word or a word of encouragement at a hard time. Just a short prayer and a kind compliment.

One of the hardest things we had to do at Combustion was fire the welder who everyone in plant 4 recognized as the world's best TIG welder. This guy made absolutely beautiful tube welds. His welds were works of art. People came by just to admire his artwork. The problem was that he would not use the high strength welding wire that was specified for the tube welds. He took soft high silicon tie wire from the tube bundles and use that for his filler metal. His welds failed in service which caused boiler outages which can cause the power to go off. Soon the Utility Companies figured out what was happening. So, he was giver an ultimatum. Stop using soft tie wire or be fired. After several days of observation, He was offered and accepted early retirement. No big going away party but he did retain his personal integrity. Few people knew the entire story. In this case the company respected the integrity of a long-term employee even though what he was doing was wrong. There are not many companies like that today. Wal-Mart is one of them.

The first Wal-Mart store in Hamilton County and one of the first in Tennessee was located in Soddy Daisy, where I lived. Not where I grew up, but I got there as soon as I could. Sam Walton, himself, showed up for the opening of the Soddy Daisy store and He stayed around for about three days. He would help people in and out of their cars and help them place their purchases into their cars. At that time everything in a Wal-Mart store was made in the USA. I ask him about that one day because US labor cost had driven a lot of manufacturing offshore. Sam said "We will only sell quality products made in the US. At a profit if we can, at a loss if we must but always quality things made in the USA. The Newport News Shipbuilding and Dry Dock Company had this the same motto. Our plan will work if I (Sam) can take care of our Associates and then our Associates will then take care of our customers." Sam's plan was good and it's working. Today Sam is not there and many of Walmart's products are made offshore. But it's still a good company like Combustion Engineering. My moto is "If Wal-Mart does not have it, I probably don't need it." There are lots of Red Smiths working at Wal-Marts. S Truett Cathy who started Chick-fil-A used a similar plan. So, if you are a Red Smith working at Wal-Mart or Chick-Fil-A or somewhere else, you are where God has placed you. Keep doing what you are doing. You don't need college, with its large student loans that you can't pay back. You surely don't need seminary; you just need Jesus. You are a missionary on a mission so just press on brother. Uncle Lester, Tony Hancock and Bill Goins never went to seminary.

Chapter 9

How to Hire a Welding Engineer

When I was working for CE Combustion Engineering my boss always wanted to be over staffed. Because when a big vessel shipped there was a good possibility that CE would initiate a shop wide lay off. It was quite common that we would lay people off one week and the next week we would be hiring workers. Late one afternoon my boss handed me a stack of resumes of welding engineers from Ingles Shipyard. He told me he had already decided who to hire buy he just wanted my input. All of these engineers were highly qualified. With welding engineering degrees from Ohio State, Rensselaer, Cal Tech. etc. They were trained by all the colleges that train good welding engineers.

To evaluate each of these highly qualified engineers would require at least a 20-minute interview. This was not possible or even necessary since my boss had already decided who we were going to hire. I looked through the stack. They were all highly qualified. With publications in the Welding Journal, ASME Journal, even one article in the prestigious European journal DVS Deutscher Verband fur SchweiBen and verwandte Verfahren e V. (The German Welding Society). How could I ignore this guy since I had also published in DVS? One resume had a single sentence that elevated one engineer above all the rest. In the comments section the author had written "I teach Sunday School". This was our man! My boss would pick him and because of that note, He was my first choice. We hired him. And we never regretted making that selection.

Three years later I laid him off. Because when the shop work drops off, we would have a lay off. No problem, welding engineers are used to being laid off and re-hired. It's part of the territory. Actually, I helped him find a better job with a better retirement package with the NRC Nuclear Regulatory Commission. It was a higher paying job then I had.

A few years later, when I was working at the TVA Sequoyah Nuclear Plant, we had a problem that NRC management decided needed some special oversight. Guess who the NRC sent in? That same Engineer that I had hired from Ingles Shipyard 20 years earlier. He was still teaching Sunday school. The inspection could have gone really bad for me and for TVA but because of the trust that I had established with this engineer, it went well.

Bottom Line: Always hire a Sunday school teacher. Uncle Lester was a Sunday school teacher for over 40 years. He taught us that.

Chapter 10

What We Have Learned About Unions

If it's made in China, I usually don't want to buy it. Unless Wal-Mart has it on the clearance isle at ½ price or less. Then I cannot resist buying it even if it was made in China. But why are so many things today made in China? Don't we know the Russians and Chinese are our enemies?

And it takes forever to get stuff from China.

There is one simple answer to this question-Labor Cost. Unions in America have driven labor cost so high that American companies, to still make a profit, have moved their factories offshore, usually to China or Mexico. A few automobile manufacturing companies still have factories in the non-union south, where state labor laws keep the unions out. An example is the Volkswagen non-union plant in Chattanooga. It's a great place to work. But if you live in Wheelwright Kentucky, you either work for the coal company if you can get in the union, or you move or you live in poverty.

One of the core principles we learned from Uncle Lester was, "do not gamble". That includes buying lottery tickets or other betting. At the Sequoyah Nuclear Plant, the union workers were constantly raffling off a verity of items. Usually knifes, shotgun, pistols, garden equipment, etc. If you had any money in your pocket, they would separate you from some of that money. So, I never had more than $3 in my wallet at any one time. I would constantly get ask "you want to buy a chance on this, knife or gun or some other men's toy. They were gamblers. The most common item offered at lottery, for just a $5 ticket, was the latest stainless steel belt buckles, manufactured on site. Almost everyone had one and if you were not wearing a fancy stainless steel belt buckle, you would sometime this week be asked to buy a raffle ticket for the latest one to be offered for lottery. Buying a lottery ticket each week was something Uncle Lester taught us not to do.

What I observed working at TVA for 29 years was that union workers slow walking was the main reason that several Nuclear Plants were never finished on schedule, any schedule. Union workers are experts at making a 20-minute job last all week and even require overtime on the weekend. It happened all the time. It was a game. Several nuclear plants were never finished mainly because the union workers slow walked the work until the utility ran out of money. It was not just TVA. Other utilities walked away from unfinished nuclear plants. The unions just slow walked the work until the utility ran out of money.

If you are in a union, you are blessed. You get high wages, health insurance, retirement, etc. But if you are not in the union you are scum. The teacher's unions is powerful example. If you are a teacher, part of their union dues goes directly to fund the democratic party. It's a bribe. If you complain you get harassed. Unions are just like the communist party, if you are inside the tent you are fat and happy. But If you are outside the tent, no one cares about you, just don't get out of line. There must ALWAYS be enough tough people inside the tent to keep those of us peons outside the tent under control. That's why the country needs electric cars, so our government can just turn off a big switch in the sky, and us peasants outside the tent, cannot travel. See the chapter on the hoax -global warming. Never buy an electric car. They can spontaneously catch on fire.

New pastors, this is not a subject you want to deal with from the pulpit! There are many subjects that should not be on your

Sunday sermon list, and unions is one to avoid at all cost. Because setting on the back pew may just be the retired job Stewart for the local IBEW. He will not understand your message and there are many other messages that he will appreciate. Politics is another subject you want to stay away from. Stick to expository preaching directly from the Bible, one book at a time. There is both good and bad in unions, mostly bad.

Chapter 11

Global Warming is a HOAX!

Global Warming is the biggest lie in recent history. It is a lie being used by the communists to destroy Americia[7]. The Global Warming HOAX has been completely examined. One book on this lie is S. Fred Singer's book "Hot Talk, Cold Science[8]. Get the third edition. This book is available from Amazon, Books A Million and many other sources. You can actually obtain a free copy by calling (800) 456-5107.

Don't just take our word for it, get the free book. And if you want near term reliable electric power you will have to move to France. Our government has declared war on fossil fuels for no reason except they are following a big lie. The state of California just stated that after a certain date, they will no longer sell cars that run on fossil Fuels (gas). This has to be one of the dumbest things to ever come out of California and they hold the record for dumbness. You want believe the stories people moving to Tennessee from California tell us.

Al Gore junior was one of the first big liberal to spread the global warming hoax. His father Al Gore senior, a senator from Tennessee, was the first big liberal that Uncle Lester taught me to vote against. Lester also told me not to tell people who I voted for because I might offend a few good men. The liberals have become experts at justifying all their social agendas on the hoax of global warming. We don't need to shut down our coal fired electric plants. The CO2 emission promotes plant growth. It's the SO2 often emitted when coal is burned that kills plants. Remove the SO2 with a scrubber and coal emissions are good for agriculture. And we sure don't need electric cars. Uncle Lester would never have bought an electric car. How dumb. And global warming is not causing weather changes.

More than 1,100 Scientists and Professionals worldwide have signed a declaration stating that "there's no climate emergency". The document has 1,152 signatures from 15 countries as of Aug 23, 2020. Of course, no government employee would sign this document because he would be immediately fired[9].

An excellent reference for understanding how communism is used the global warming lie to promote their worldwide agenda is "How the Specter of Communism is Ruling the World" published by The Epic Times[7].

Ultimately it comes down to our communism's attempt to control how we will live our life in the coming years.

Some other references are:

http://www.wnho.net/global_warming.htm
http://magicvalley.com/news/opinion/mailbag/letter-to-the-editor-global-warming-hoax-designed-to-scare/article_3a4e1815-7acc-59af-bb8f-1a423d1495da.html

http://americandailyherald.com/pundits/chris-clancy/item/the-great-global-warming-swindle

Chapter 12

Boundary Water Canoe Area

The Boundary Waters Canoe Area is 8 million acers of wilderness on the US-Canadian border. It is one of the most sparsely populated areas in the world. No roads, no cabins, no stores, nothing but lakes and islands. The only access is by canoe or float plane. The only communication is by satellite phone. Our group of eight paddlers (4 adults and 4 teenagers) were on a 7-day, 100-mile adventure. Ninety miles paddling, 10 miles portaging. The portages are the hard part. It was early on day four. We had been paddling for about 2 hours. Four Canoes in a straight line, 2 paddlers per canoe. I was in the lead boat and my paddling buddy Jamie, was more interested in eating prunes and throwing the seed in the water than paddling. It was a clear calm day with no wind and the water was like a sheet of clear glass. There was no sound except the strokes of our paddles and a distant Loon. Loons make a lot of noise. As Jamie threw a prune seed into the air, a musky jumped out of the water and caught the seed in midair. We both got wet. Since we were in the lead canoe everyone saw the fish jump out of the water. Everyone wanted to stop paddling and start musky fishing. With prune seeds of course. The descriptions of how long that fish was varied from "longer than the canoe," "over 25 feet" "etc." But it was probably about 30 inches long. We did not stop to fish because we had 18 miles to go that day. In the Boundary Waters you have to camp in a designated camp site each night. Our destination was still a long way off.

About an hour later, I spotted a group on a small hill directly ahead of us. In the Boundary Waters there are very few people. If you see 2 fishermen, it's a crowded day. You want to stop and talk. This crew I had spotted looked different. I asked the group who were not paying attention, "Hey guys don't that look like a bunch of girls on that hill? "At which point paddlers became energized. Three canoes went into instant 4-wheel drive. I was the last canoe to get to the shore. It appeared that these girls were gathered around something and looking across the lakes. Actually, they were lost and had been lost for 2 days. After passing this same place, this hill, for the third time they decided to climb up the hill and see if they could figure out where they were by studying their map. Its common when you are lost to go in circles and that is what they were doing.

When I got out for my canoe, after the rest of our crew had charged up the hill to meet our new friends, I picked up my map. These girls looked beat.

The first thing their leader said to me was "Do you know where we are?"

I answered her "In the Boundary Waters." That was not the answer she was looking for. I quickly found out that they were a Girl Scout Troop from Indiana and had been on many canoe trips. But this was their first trip to the Boundary Water. So how could a competent, experienced, very intelligent group get so badly lost? There was one thing missing from their navigation skills. The Iron ore content in the lakes makes a compass worthless. Actually, their compass is what got them lost. If you place your compass on the seat in front of you as you paddle, you will see the needle swing back and forth due to the iron ore deposits. These girls did not understand what iron does to a compass. Thus, they got lost.

They had planned to catch fish and had not packed a lot of extra food but because of the stress of being lost they had not fished. Thus, they were almost out of food. We had caught lots of fish. Mostly bass and walleye, a few saggars but no musky, except the one Jamie enticed with a prune seed. We had two Duluth packs of food that we did not need. So, we gave them enough food to get them back to their border crossing. They were two lake chains off from where they needed to be to get to their designated Border Crossing. They had 2 hard days of paddling. A hard trip but doable.

We exited Canada at a different border crossing, so I never found out if they got out or died in the wilderness. But I think they got out and on schedule. The Canadian Mounties will not even come look for you until you are late for 3 days. I could not get the Mounty at our crossing interested in my story. But he did promise to call the other check point when the satellite phone was working. We did not know, and the Girl Scouts did not know that some of the communication satellites were dead. You could only make a call when a live satellite was over head. The outfitter should have given us a chart showing us when we could make calls. The phone worked great the first night we used it but after that we never could make a call.

So, what's the takeaway?

1. Never go into the wilderness without someone who has been there before. The navigation skills that you used on the last trip may just get you lost. Know the territory.

2. If you see a group that looks like they need help, especially if it's a group of women, stop and help them. If God had not scheduled us to be on that lake at that time, their story would have had a different ending.

3. No matter how hard you work, if your compass is pointed in the wrong direction you will remain lost. If these girls had just looked up at the Big Dipper and found the North Star that God placed in the sky for them, they would not have stayed lost.

4. If you are depending on a satellite phone, know when the live satellites are overhead.

5. In America have we lost our moral compass? Why is all this happening to America? Deuteronomy 29:29 provides us some insight "The secret things belong to the Lord our God, but the things revealed belong to us and to our children forever, that we may follow all the words of this law." When we took the Bibles out of our schools, we lost our moral vision (Compass) as a Nation because we no longer teach the word of God to our children.

6. I learned to fish from (you guessed it) Uncle Lester.

Chapter 13

Church Structure That Works!

Pastors this chapter may be the most important one in this book! The best way to organize any church is to follow Dr. Bill Blanchard's book entitled *Church Structure That Works* ISBN 978-1-935265-23-8 Second Edition. But don't make, even small changes, too soon. As Dr Blanchard explains in his book, a Baptist church needs 3 strong committees. One to watch the money, one to watch the staff and one to nominate members to the committees and jobs. There are other important committees, the Deacons, the Trustees and those groups that promote missions, social events, children's programs, VBS, music and sound. These are all important but the money watchers, the staff watchers and the committee stackers are the big 3. If these three areas are covered, the church will run smoothly. When members have a concern or a need and they learn that they can just go to one of these 3 groups to get their questions answered or their need met, your church will run smooth. And you don't have to micro-manage every church detail. They will like church better and you will like church better. Actually, you won't even hear about some of the issues. Some criticize Bill Blanchard's' approach because they say that committees are not mentioned in the New Testament. They may be right but if you find a better way to organize a church, let us know.

One caution, if someone offers you a check book, run from that temptation. Tell them to check out "The Demise of the Two Rivers Baptist Church, Nashville." This story is documented in detail on Wartburg Watch[11]. Two Rivers was the largest Baptist Church in Middle Tennessee. Today it is a

Catholic facility, because no one was watching the money. Don't ever touch the money. You do not want to know how much any member donates to the church. Do not ask.

Another interesting story is the collapse of Mega church Highland Park Baptist and Tennessee Temple University after long-term Pastor Dr. Lee Robinson died[12].

It is important for you to get to know the man who served as the church's Interim Pastor before you got there. If he was there any time at all, he will know the congregation. Actually, some members will have become so attached to this Interim pastor that they wanted him to have your job. This group will actually go to him with comments that they will not share with you. It's a good idea to have lunch each month with the old Interim. He is probably one of your biggest friends and can be one of your greatest prayer supporters. Invite him back to special events. Keep him in the loop. Especially for funerals and weddings.

If you are going to your first pastorate, or if you have recently moved to a new congregation, you will quickly learn who the church power brokers are. They will let you know exactly how things work and that any change will not work unless their blessing is up on it. The problem may be as simple as moving a choir chair on the platform or changing the order of service, to take up the offering at a different time. But you will know quickly that they are unhappy. It's interesting that quite often these big shot power brokers are not long-term members of the church. They may be relatively new in this church and a little checking will reveal that they caused similar hate and discontent in their former church. Quit often these self-anointed power brokers will just move on to another church where they become someone else's problem. You may need to consider some appropriate biblical church discipline after much prayer.

Quickly determine who the long-term members of the church are. They are the real source of spiritual strength, but they don't say much.

Another very important thing is that unless the church you are going to is very small, there are other staff members there already. Some have been there for years. They can either be your best supporters or your worst enemies. That's why you must get to know all of the current staff during the interview process. You may someday meet a staff member that you just can't stand. It's best to identify that person before you accept the call. The Baptist Association's Director of Missions is a good source to help you navigate the bumps in this road. Because he knows the landscape. If a church has hired and fired 3 pastors in the last 6 years, something bad is going on. You may not want that church. But if God is calling you there, go but you may be traveling a road like Peter, Lucy, and Susan on their way to Narnia.

The Church Business Meeting are for conduction business not a place to chase rabbits. Not a time for complaining or griping. Your church parliamentarian, if your new church has a parliamentarian, should control the business meetings in accordance with Roberts Rules of Order which is all about business. If you are not formular with Roberts Rules, you should get a copy and read it. When you attend your first Annual Southern Baptist Convention you will see Roberts Rules in action. Your Business Meetings should be no longer than one hour.

Your first Deacons Meeting may be a lot longer than one hour. Actually, deacons' meetings have been known to start at 7 pm and go past midnight. This is the time for chasing rabbits and resolving complaints. Resolve all issues before you adjourn.

At your first deacons meeting ask, "Are there any Eagle scouts in the room?" Usually, one hand will go up. Then ask "did we ever have Boy Scout here? "Then ask have we considered starting a Trail Life USA or American Heritage group here? Follow the group, if no one will step up to lead it, let it die for now.

Chapter 14

The Gym that We Could Not Afford

Many Pastors get in trouble because they take on a building project that their church cannot afford. FBCSD did that 10 years ago when the pastor insisted on building a gym. A neighborhood gym was actually a great idea because the elementary schools in North Hamilton County all had auditoriums but no gyms. Actually, a group from the Tennessee Baptist Convention was invited to come to FBC Soddy Daisy and evaluated our financial situation, and they recommended that we not build the gym. They said we would never pay for it, and they were right. Years later we still owe $60,000 on the gym. The plan was that after we build a gym where all the elementary school's kids could play basketball and volleyball free, and after their families visited our new gym, they would be so impressed that their family would join our church. It never happened. There was not one family that I know of, that joined the church following their use of the gym. Pastors watch the money and don't spend more than your church can pay for. After 10 years the loan was finally paid off.

Rechoboth Baptist down the road, just built a new sanctuary debt free because they raised all the money before they dug the first hole. Uncle Lester taught us that if you don't have the money don't buy it.

Chapter 15

How to Raise Children?

Use the Bible stupid. This chapter is short because I believe that there are only two sources of biblical parenting rules outside of the Bible itself. That's John Roseman[13] and Focus on the Family.[14] If King Solomon could have installed even a small part of the wisdom he wrote into the Psalms and Proverbs into his son Jeroboam, maybe the nation of Israel would not have been divided and eventually destroyed by first the Assyrians and then the Babylonians. Remember that the capital of Assyria was Nineveh. That's where Jonah was going when he was delayed by an adventure with a whale (big fish). Remember that story? You must share this with your grandkids. Just a few years later, the Assyrians had obviously forgotten everything Jonah taught them. Later, Amos tried to warn the nation of Israel, but it was too late.

If Solomon had just been able to read and apply some of the principles in John Roseman's book "The Bible Parenting Code"[13] history could have been different. But you still have time to write your own history. And direct your children and the children in your church. John Roseman will come to your church and train you and your people. Call him. If you don't do anything else, read chapter 29 of his book and apply it! "Because You Say So!" based on Ephesians 6:1 "Children, obey your parents in the Lord, for this is good."

As John Roseman so clearly explains in him book, your role as a husband or wife is much more important than your role as a parent. Do not spend all your time focused on your children. The correct ratio is 20% of your effort focused on the chile and 80% focused on your spouse. God created you to be a husband or wife first and a to be a mother second[13].

Never try to negotiate with a two-year old. You will always loose and the two-year old will grow up to be a spoiled brat. Just say "We are doing this this way because I said so." There are many spoiled brats coming out of our public education system today who are rapidly becoming disinclined to work. 2 Thessalonians 3:10 says "If anyone is not willing to work, he should not eat".

Never feed a spoiled brat. It's best that they die young. (just kidding). But you will want to die after your kid become an adult and continue to behave like they are still two-year- old.

Chapter 16

How to Pray for Your children!

In Appendix 1 are *31 Biblical Virtues that you should Pray for your Child.*[9] Fourth on this list is "Willingness to Work" The prayer reads — Teach my children Lord to value work and to work with all their heart. As working for the Lord and not for men. (Col 3:23). As explained earlier, America is on a rapid path to become a nation where our people are becoming disinclined to work. That must be turned around. This country was founded on hard work.

Does the church you are considering have a group of prayer warriors involved in programs like "Moms in Tough" or D group. If not ask why not? Their answer may help you decide that this is not the church for you.

Pastors you can make the difference. But prayer makes the most difference.

Chapter 17

Trip to Russia

What's it like in Russia and what is it going to be like in America in 50 years if something big does not change?

I few years ago, I had the opportunity to visit southern Russia for a week. Actually, we were going to visit about 60 miles from the Ukraine border. It takes a lot of preparation to visit a communist country. We studied the language, applied for pass ports and visas and had to submit a detailed plan for what, where, when and how everything would flow. Our leader, Jimmy, had been there before and had made friends with a preacher in small church in Southern Russia. Yes, there are a few small churches in Russia. We spent weeks learning the Russian language, which I felt was hard to learn and we would each have a translator. Some meals would be eaten in the hotel, but many meals would be eaten in the pastor's small home. We had to take enough money to purchase the food we would eat and also food for the Pastors family and the visitors that the pastor always invited to eat with us. There was typically about 25 people in his 900 square foot house. Everything is very compact in Russia. After we had raised enough money for the trip, I ask Jimmy "how much money do we have left, I need to buy bibles." He said, "I don't know how much is here" and he handed me a hand full of money. I did not count it. But the next day I went to see Spiros Zodhiates, director of AMG ministries, in Chattanooga. They publish bibles. I told him what we were doing and ask him to sell me some new leather-bound Russian translations bibles. I still had not counted the money. He took my hand full of money, did not count it, handed it to his secretary, went out in the warehouse and handed me a case of new leather-bound Russian translation bibles. I packed them in the bottom of my extra suitcase. The top of the suitcase was stuffed with teddy bears because we were scheduled to visit a state-run orphanage where the kids, we were told, had never had a teddy bear.

God would have to get those bibles and bears through customs at the Moscow airport. Both items are strictly prohibited from entering Russia.

At customs I had two bags. I presented my personal bag first which contained only clothes for a week. The agent looked at every item in my bag. Then I presented my second bag, and he ask me "what's in this bag, it was heavy. I told him it was teddy bears that we were giving to orphans in an orphanage. His face changed when I told him the bag contained teddy bears. As He started to pull the zipper, one of the bears legs shot out of the opening. He stopped, pushed the leg back into the opening, closed the zipper and said in a gruff voice, "Get out of here". God had gotten his word through customs. Here's why. At the housing project where we were giving away, new leather bound, Russian language bibles that you can go to Jail for just having one in your possession, as we handed a bible to an elderly lady, she dropped down on her knees and started screaming in Russian. We did not know what she was saying. But soon found out she had been saved 40 years earlier and had been praying for her own bible for over 40 years. God answers her prayer. We had the honor of delivering the bible, and we got the blessing.

Where we were in Southern Russia you could own a car and you could drive around inside that town, but you could not leave town. All roads out of town were guarded 24 hours a day by armed guards to keep people from entering or leaving the town. Three days before we were scheduled to leave by train, we sent our passports by courier to the train station to Apply for permission to leave town. A bribe was expected to accompany the application. In Russia the people cannot travel freely.

If everyone in America drove an electric car, our government could program our cars so you could not leave town. When you drove to the town boundary, the car computer would just shut off the car. Do you now understand why our government is so focused on electric cars. It's control. America is becoming just like Russia. The goal of Biden's recent executive order funding biotechnology and biomanufacturing is to allow our government in the future to program us so we will have no desire to go anywhere. That's scarry.

Pastor, can you foresee an America where you can not own a Bible? I can. If the Marxist-promoting liberals continue on the path they are leading us America will become just like Russia. Bibles have been removed from most of our public schools. But not in Hamilton County Tennessee. What's next? Uncle Lester always had his Bible near his phone so if someone called him with a question, he could look up the answer. The liberals plan is to first take the Bibles out of our schools, so our kids can't read it and then take the bibles out of our homes. Gideons need to be standing on the Mexican border giving a bible, in their heart language, to everyone crossing the border. Donald Trump will likely pay for the bibles after he gets re-elected President in November 2022.

Do you see it? America can become just like Russia and China.

Chapter 18

Ugly Bicycle

There are few places in America where the poverty level is lower than in Wheelwright Kentucky, coal mining country. There are a few jobs in the remaining mines and those are union jobs that pay well. Miners drive new trucks. There are a few teaching jobs and a few jobs at the nearby prison. But the majority of the people there live-in severe poverty.

I was loading the 16-foot covered trailer with suppliers for the Wheelwright Mission Center. Donations had been dropped off from several local churches and several items purchased from the local wall mart. This trailer was going to be full. Someone had dropped off a 20- inch boys' bicycle that had not been well cared for. I remember thinking that this had to be the ugliest bicycle in Chattanooga. My kids would not ride it, it was just too ugly. But it had good tires. I just set it aside.

After all the supplies were loaded and the trailer was almost full, there was a small gap in the top near the rear door. Just enough room to slide in that ugly bicycle. So, I slid the bike in the top of the trailer.

When I backed into the mission center, I noticed a young boy setting by the center door. The first thing I removed from the trailer was that ugly bicycle. He saw it and ask me, "Mister are you going to sell that bicycle?" I answered, "no we are going to give it away." He asks, "can I have it?". I told him to go ask Mr. Wilson. He flew into the building, can back quickly and told me "He said I could have it." Then I said, "It's yours."

He jumped on that ugly bicycle and started riding up the mountain road saying, "I got to show this to mama."

What I had misjudged as something too ugly to give away, God had used as a valuable gift to a young boy. We can never know the full impact of our acts of kindness.

Chapter 19

Widows, Deacons and Other Special Groups

Every church has several groups that need special attention from their Pastor.

Acts chapter 6 describes the needs of some widows in the early church. Actually, this is where Deacons got started. Howard Forshee[16] in his Book "Now You are a Deacon "states that the most important roll of the deacons is to minister to Widows. If the church you are considering does not have an active ministry to their widows, you may want to keep looking. You will need a copy of this book for each deacon.

Veterans should receive special attention. An annual Veterans dinner open to the community is a great time to connect to the community outside the church. Several of your church members have relatives that never returned from WWII, Korea, Vietnam, etc. Many will come to a veteran's dinner just for the fellowship.

Shut-in meals are an excellent Sunday School outreach. Usually, once a month take a meal to each shut-in family. Call them first to verify that they are going to be home, and that they don't have special dietary needs. They will enjoy the visit more than the meal.

While an annual veteran's meal will have great outreach benefits, avoid weekly community meals. Following a tornado disaster in Chattanooga several churches opened their doors to provide free meals both to the homeowners whose houses were damaged but also to the relief workers that came to provide support. That was a great short-term ministry. But free community meals should not be offered on a long-term basis. While community meals are a bad idea, food bank is a good idea if done right. The National Food Bank program is a good way to feed lots of hungry people in your community. While the food that you get from the federal food bank is not all free, it is doable for your church, if your church has enough volunteers to staff the program. Actually, you will have members of other churches coming to help in your Food Bank. Food Bank is very labor intensive. Proceed with caution. The fields may be ripe, but the workers are few.

Chapter 20

Rich Strike- 2022 Kentucky Derby

Rich Strike better known as Richie, by his trainers, won the 2022 Kentucky Derby by hard work[17]. Eric Reed was Rich Strike's trainer. His hard work paid off.

The race strategy used by Eric Reed was the same strategy that Roger Banister used to beat John Landy in 1954. Roger Banister was the first runner to break the 4-minute mile. His time was 3.59.4 minutes. But Just 46 days later John Landy of Australia broke that record with a time of 3.57.9 minutes. The current mile world record holders are Hicham El Guerrouj of Morocco with a time of 3:43.13 and Sifan Hassan of The Netherlands holds the women's record of 4:12.33 minutes.

In 1954 in Vancouver, a race between Roger Banister and John Landy was to determine who really was the world's fastest runner. John Landy's strategy was to jump out in front early and run hard. Roger Banister's strategy was to run steady until near the end and then turn on the speed. Very near the end of the race John Landy still had a small lead. But he could hear Roger Banister closing behind him. As he looked back to see how much lead he had, Roger Banister passed him. Banister's win was due to his hard work at the finish line.

Rich Strikes' win in the 2022 Kentucky Derby was based on this same strategy. Rich Strike ran in the back of the pack until near the end of the race, then he turned on the speed. Passing every horse in the race. It was hard work.

Bottom line run steady most of your race but turn on the speed when near the finish line or when it's important. There are many events (races) in life that you can walk through. But there are other important races that require all your attention and effort. The effort required on these important races will require hard work. You cannot run every race in life using the same strategy.

Bottom line- we knew that Rich Strike could win, and we understood what the payoff would be. But we did not place a bet, because Uncle Lester taught us to never bet on a racehorse.

Chapter 21

A Big Land Deal That Was Missed

About 1918 one of our relatives Lee Boykin missed a big land deal. Lee owned a tire store in Bradley county Tennessee. He had a near monopoly on tires but there were not many cars back then. He had saved a rather large sum to invest. At the advice of a trusted friend, he drove a Model T Ford from Cleveland Tennessee to Miami Florida. A simple 800-mile trip today. He went to look at a possible land investment. The trip took 4 days of hard driving each way. There were no good roads. He had 5 flat tires going down and 7 flat tires on the return. No air condition in a black car. All of Henry Ford's cars were black.

The prize investment was undeveloped flat land across the road from Miami Beach selling for $10 per archer. He could have bought a large part of Miami Beach that day. And he had the money in his pocket. He brought a lot of cash with him to invest. He bought nothing.

Every time Lee told me this story, which was about every time I saw him about 40 years later, He would almost cry. I believed the story because he always told it exactly the same way and each time, he would almost cry.

So how did this successful businessman miss such a great investment? Lee reasoned that since it had taken him 4 days to drive to this beautiful place, no one would ever drive that far for vacation. Owning beautiful wilderness that far away would be a bad investment he thought. He did not envision the interstate highway system that Dwight Eisenhour would build following WWII.

Contrast that to what our Uncle Lester did. He sold his first car, which had been given to him to drive Ressie to school, for a school bus. Then he used that school bus as a down payment for a filling station. Then he used the filling station as a down payment for his first farm. And every time adjacent farmland became available, he bought it. He eventually accumulated several hundred acers of farmland with several houses and barns. Uncle Lester was eventually inducted into the Bradley County Agriculture Hall of Fame.

Bottom line- If you can buy land, buy it. Buying land is not like buying a Tennessee lottery ticket. After the drawing, you will still have something to stand on. Don't wait for the government to build a bridge to your place.

Chapter 22

Dental Tools can only be used as designed.

My younger son Clay is a children's dentist. That path took 4 years at Murray State, 4 years at the University of Tennessee Medical School, and 2 years at University of Kentucky Pediatric Dental school. That's 10 years of college. I am proud of him and his hard work. You can travel that path if you are so called but it's a long path to ministry. He did and it is a very rewarding path. The question is can you walk this path without student loans. That's not important if you plan to practice dentistry like Clay did. Because you can eventually earn enough to pay off those loans. But if you are headed for Ministry on a small church staff, like most young pastors, it will be very difficult to pay back those student loans.

Here is the bottom line: Dental tools are designed to perform specific jobs. The dentist will ask his assistant to hand him a specific tool. After the dentist and assistant have worked together for some time the assistant will know which tool is next and hand it to the dentist before he asks for it. Never will the assistant hand the dentist a tool and suggest that it be used for an application other that what it was designed for. That will not work.

You the reader, have been designed by God for a specific job (ministry). That's why you are reading this book. If you are not working in the roll that God has called you to, you are miserable. You are like the dental tool. You will not be happy until you are working where God has called you.

Chapter 23

Divorce

Pastors you probably already know that you will spend a lot of happy time conducting marriages. Actually, in most states, you cannot sign a marriage certificate until you are licensed by that state. Some state laws are changing to allow non-ordained people (men and women) to conduct marriage services.

Marriage is hard work. Probably one of the hardest jobs of all. That's why when the going gets rough it's just too easy to get divorced. Divorce is a tough animal. And usually a very bad animal. Greedy lawyers' milk the system. Some Lawyers have told me that they will not take a divorce case because it's just too hard to deal with two people who now hate each other when just a short time ago they testified in church that they Loved each other. It's just too hard. They are not willing to do the hard work. And the greatest hurt goes to the children if there are any. And the grandparents of those children.

What is happening in America? Kent Evens at Manhood Journey[17] says:

1. 19.5 million children live without a father at home

2. 746,971 marriages ended in divorce last year

3. 1.2 million students dropped out of school

Divorce is killing America. Especially black Americans. People have become disinclined to work. So, what can a new Pastor do? First of all, if you don't know them, don't marry them. No matter how hard they try to convince you that they love each other. Especially if they have big student loans. All the people in divorce cases in America started out thinking that they loved each other. They took vows in church "to love and cherish until death do us part". When trouble comes, they quickly change their mind. It's too much work.

Take a class in "Divorce Care". That's a subject that most seminaries don't cover. But many denominations have excellent training in this very important area. You may need to take one of Ron Blues courses in financial management, because money flow (creating it, dividing it, spending it, and saving it) is the biggest issue in divorce. Especially if there are kids involved.

Years ago, I was doing door to door visitation with my good friend and pastor Danny Prior. We knocked on a door and the lady immediately recognized Danny as the pastor who had conducted her marriage. Then Danny said something that was absolutely the dumbest words to ever come out of a visitation pastor's mouth. He asks, "Did the marriage work?" Since we know that fifty percent of all marriages fail, asking that question has a 50% probably of a "no" answer. Which is exactly what he got. I share this story with you, so you will not make this same mistake.

I got to add one important caution about same sex marriage. It your church has a center aisle and a large seating capacity; you will eventually be approached by a same sex couple wanting to exchange their vows in your church. Be Prepared. Most states have revised their laws to require you to let then in, unless your church's constitution and by-laws specifically forbid it. Check with a lawyer to make sure you are currency with your state laws. This is a good way to get fired.

Chapter 24

Scripture and Nature

Love Letters from the Same God

NOTE: This Chapter Was Written by John Burkitt. It is used with permission from the Author

If one of the elders of the church comes up to you and asks, "Why do we need a Trail Life Troop," what will you say? You might start off with the unique role of outdoor adventure ministry.

Why outdoor adventure ministry

Progressives have pushed Christianity out of schools, politics, and the justice system. Traditional Christianity is incompatible with their vision of the future...a future involving our children. It's time we pushed back. Let's step out into the sunshine to harness the power of outdoor adventure ministry. More than ever, boys need outdoor adventure with God. This is in addition to their need for Church and Sunday School. It poses new challenges and opens new opportunities for your church. When God breathed into Adam, he joined the natural with the supernatural. Our relationship with nature is a vital part of who we are and how we serve God. Just as Scripture reveals the spiritual side of Christianity, Nature reveals the physical side. God wants us to be His people in body as well as spirit. The supernatural side of Christianity has wide appeal. Loving one another, not judging, and sharing eternal life are as crowd pleasing today as they were in Jesus' time. "Faith" sounds harmless. The natural side of Christianity is the hard sell. Self-denial and absolute truth do not fit in with the modern spirit. Obedience sounds costly…and it can be.

Yet Nature and Scripture are liberating, not confining. We should answer their call to "respect authority and be a good steward of creation," to choose God and life over sin and death. And so, we teach Trailmen a timeless values system: to manage resources, revere nature, love our neighbors, and worship God. That is the Heart of the Outdoors, and the Heart of Trail Life. "That sounds right," the elder says, "but what can you find in the woods that you can't find in the Bible?"

How does outdoor adventure ministry work?

Special revelation is God's truth conveyed through Scripture. Churches are skilled in its use, with more than 2000 years of experience. General Revelation is God's truth conveyed through nature. For many churches, this is a new frontier in ministry, and at first it can feel intimidating. Nature is not a substitute for scripture, but neither is scripture a substitute for nature; they complement each other. We must leverage both for our children. Without scripture, nature comes across as a battleground for conflicting powers that charm us, then lash us with tempests, tigers, and spears. Without nature, scripture becomes a belief system you could assent to like casting a vote for Jesus. If creation and experience did not matter, faith without works would be alive. Scripture and Nature were designed to reveal aspects of God's wisdom, power, and righteousness over the course of our lives. They are God's love letters to people of matter and spirit. "Movies only seem real in the theater. If the church becomes a theater, God becomes a movie. He must always be everywhere. We mustn't put God in a box." "Why not find out for yourself? Troop 317 meets at Johnson City Baptist Church. I've been volunteering there for two years, and they'd love to see you this Tuesday at 7:00."

Reflecting and connecting

Nature in a Scriptural Context You proudly wear the uniform, and you want to make a difference through Trail Life. Great! So, how do you harness the power of outdoor adventure ministry?

Scripture through the lens of nature sets us many fine examples. It is truthful, faithful, humbling, orderly, appropriate, and indwelling. — Our Actions have direct consequences that reflect eternal truths about life. — God's faithful promises to the sleeping seed and the hibernating bear are a foretaste of our own promised resurrection.

Nature humbles us, revealing our weakness and dependence. Its scale, detail, redundancy, and permanence made King David ask God, "What is man that Thou art mindful of him?" — Nature is orderly, designed by God with nothing lacking and nothing wasted. Intelligent design is apparent in every detail. — Nature is an appropriate environment for us, made by our Creator and placed under our stewardship. — Our indwelling spiritual and physical nature testifies to God's wisdom, power, and love. In short, Nature focuses Scripture by demonstrating how God translated spiritual ideas into material order and pattern. And God saw all that He had made, and behold, it was very good. – Genesis 1:31a

Nature through the lens of scripture

Scripture is the divine perspective on nature—including human nature. It is focused, targeted, timeless, hopeful, and qualitative. — Scripture does not correct the evidence of God in nature--it focuses our vision. — It does not answer all our questions; it targets the important ones, bringing us to salvation, not civilization. — Scripture is timeless, speaking to yesterday's shepherds and tomorrow's astronauts by not linking evangelism to science. — It commands us to be good stewards of creation as it is today, lessened by our sin, making us hopeful that we will share in its original splendor. — It reveals qualities of the wonders and complexities of nature that go beyond usefulness and transcend mere beauty. In short, Scripture points us to a perfect existence that nature once had and will have again someday. For we know that the whole creation groans and suffers the pains of childbirth together until now. And not only that, but also, we ourselves, having the first fruits of the Spirit, even we ourselves groan within ourselves, waiting eagerly for our adoption as sons and daughters, the redemption of our body. – Romans 8:22

"Soaking" or "proclaiming" vs. "interpreting"

"Outdoor Adventure Ministry" sounds like a balancing act. In a way it is. On the one side, who are we to second-guess the clarity of God in nature? Won't the Trailmen pick up on it by themselves? Not necessarily. Soaking is surrounding yourself with the clues for intelligent design without putting them into context. You may try to find Jesus in a field of flowers, but the ancients had flowers and found different gods there with different values. Cultures without the lens of scripture blamed the tempests of nature on poor workmanship and divine arrogance. On the other side, should you avoid soaking by having a Bible verse ready for every occasion? No. Proclaiming is imposing scriptural evidence over the natural evidence. If you obscure God's fingerprints on creation, that is a form of religious activity, but it is not outdoor adventure ministry. It is tempting to put our own spin on nature, especially when we are feeling inexperienced, impatient, or insecure. That's what training and practice are for, to help you grow beyond that. Nature has its own authentic voice and plenty to say about God, beauty, and the meaning of life. Linger, look, listen, and learn. Is balance achieved by quoting scripture sometimes and not at others? Or does the answer not lie between soaking and proclaiming? Balance comes from Interpreting, allowing nature and scripture to work together to reveal God. Interpreting is true outdoor adventure ministry. Interpreting does not blame nature or God for our fallen world. It lets creation speak for itself, properly focused by the lens of scripture. Its message is balanced, both ancient and timely. But ask the animals and they will teach you, or the birds in the sky and they will tell you; or speak to the earth, and it will teach you, or let the fish in the sea inform you. Which of all these does not know that the hand of the Lord has done this? -- Job 12:7-10 The sermon is an important summarizing act of worship on Sunday morning. It takes a step toward formal worship, yet it should have a rustic flavor consistent with what came before.

Reflecting and connecting

On a well-run outing, your program day is spent in physical activities which provide experience—the raw material of evangelism, and the source of clues for intelligent design. Later, you process experiences and examine clues, providing them with context from the Scriptures. Your plan is to reflect on the day's events and connect them to God's perfect plan. Bees gathering nectar get covered in pollen, but it doesn't interfere with their work. Outdoor adventure ministry gracefully unites the nectar of adventure with the pollen of ministry. When bees find a good source of nectar, they go back to the hive and tell the others. When Trailmen find adventure, they gladly tell their friends. The pollen spreads, and so do the flowers. Thus, Christ's body grows ever bigger and brighter. We live in a world of shadows that needs all the light it can get. Scripture and Nature are honest lights that pierce the shadows to reveal matter and spirit as they really are, and so reveal God. They also reveal the traps our young folk must learn to avoid. "I believe in Christianity as I believe that the sun has risen not only because I see it, but because by it I see everything else." - C. S. Lewis Reflecting and Connecting is a skill like knot-tying that gets better with practice. It is the heart and soul of outdoor adventure ministry, and you will want it in your Troop.

Challenges and opportunities

Finding Certainty in a Skeptical Age

We looked at focusing nature through the lens of scripture, and scripture through the lens of nature. There is another way people try to bring the world into focus... a way without God.

The created vs. The emerged

Today's culture is a battleground of two incompatible philosophies for the hearts and souls of our children. Created Worldview — First came the PLAN, then the MAN — Good is a STANDARD — You HAVE worth from God Emerged Worldview — First came the MAN, then the PLAN — Good is a CONSENSUS — You EARN worth by deeds. Which road will our children take? God left them some clear road signs. Though you can change a light bulb by "googling" it or watching a video, God's truth is found in scripture and nature. We live in a world we built, where the stories we tell ourselves seem real. We need to venture out of it. In the works of God's hands, we find truth that will convict us but also pardon.

The spring hiking trip

Mr. Brown's Trail Life troop went for a spring hike. The weather was chilly, but the Trailmen were prepared. More importantly, Mr. Brown was prepared for outdoor ministry. In the pastoral beauty of the flowering meadow, a herd of deer carefully eyed the passing Troop. They decide it is not a threat and do not run, yet they remain alert. As they near the margin of the wood, they hear the songs of birds. There is chattering of love and new life. There are also a few sharp, scolding notes… "Scat! Go find your own territory!" At a fork in the trail, the leaders check the map. One younger Trailman idly retrieves his compass, but the decision is made by orienting the map to the lay of the land. They are well trained. They go through a rather desolate stretch of blackened and fallen trees. A fire had gone through that grove seven years ago. Still, one of the leaders points out a healthy new pine seedling. They reach the scenic overlook that is the highlight of the trail. Mr. Brown has seen it before, but he smiles. Some of the younger boys are seeing it for the first time with their Patrol friends. After the Troop returns to the campsite, evening dims the sky, and the first stars peek out. Trailmen circle the campfire to have a Trail Life "minute of ministry." What will they share?

Using reflecting and connecting

"Didn't we have a wonderful day?" Mr. Brown asks. "I got chilly last night, yet God keeps his promise that the sun will rise. And any day that begins with bacon and eggs outdoors is great." "I love watching God remake the world every spring. He always keeps his promise to the twigs, seeds, and bulbs that every winter will become spring. Ours is a God of new beginnings." "Don't forget the burned forest," said Mr. Green.

As Troop Chaplain, he tended to be very thoughtful. "Ours is also a God of new life. Even a soul scorched with sin can bloom again." Just then, young Nathan made an observation that was sharper than his grammar skills. "I learned in school that plants breathe in the air that animals breathe out. And the other way too." Mr. Green chuckled. "God helps plants with animals that provide carbon dioxide and helps animals with plants that give oxygen. They live together and rely on each other in God's perfect plan." "Remember the birds? God, who is love, made acts like raising a family enjoyable rather than ways to avoid punishment. So Trailmen, how else does He show that he loves us?"

Bert, the First Officer, pointed up at the Big Dipper. "I like that He helps us find our way. We have stars and the sun to help us. But we also have the compass when it's cloudy." Mr. Brown agreed. "God helps us travel and tell time. He also provides us the presence of His Holy Spirit to give us a different sort of guidance on a different sort of journey...life." The chaplain was feeling thoughtful. "Today was beautiful, even the sapling among the ashes.

This beauty makes us happy, even though it does not contribute to our survival." He added, "These things are evidence we were made to enjoy a world where survival and fitness are not the point. They are glimpses of the joys to come for those who believe." Reflecting and connecting gracefully sets the tone for more traditional forms of worship like singing, sharing, or group prayer requests. Mr. Brown is going to do some storytelling... "God has two houses...the small house he calls a church where we gather on Sundays, and the big house he calls the world. The world was designed and built by God, and it's quite unique..." "There are raccoons in the kitchen, otters in the bathtub, foxes in the living room, and owls in the rafters that will hoot all night. And why? Because God made them and said they were good." "It is up to us as good stewards of creation to care for them and see great truths about God and his glory in the wonders of nature..." And that is the heart of a great outing, spending the day in bold adventure, collecting the evidence of God as you go, then reflecting on that evidence and connecting it to God's word.

Chapter 25

Don't Do Stupid

Pastors, Thom Rainer[18] has identified 4 stupid areas that will get you fired. They are:

1. Flirting dangerously with Sexual boundaries

2. Plagiarism

3. Financial Stupidity

4. Social Media Madness

It should be obvious that these 4 areas will get you fired. And you are only allowed one failure in this vocation. So read Thom's list, study these areas, pray about these areas and don't do stupid.

Chapter 26

After you get your first Preaching Job

"If you happen to follow an effective Interim pastor, he will have loosened the soil, removed some of the rocks and weeds, and planted healthy seeds in the staff garden". See Barbara Child's book "In the Interim", page 89

Otherwise tread lightly. Read and understand the Church Covenant and Bi Laws.

—Don't make major changes early.

—Don't move the Deacons meeting to a different night. Read the last 2 years deacon meeting minutes.

—Don't cancel Sunday night services or change the time for Wednesday Night programs.

—Don't coach a ball team

—Don't change the music by eliminating the choir and introduce praise music only.

—Attend SBC, State Baptist Annual meetings and Local Baptist Association Annual meetings and encourage lay members to go with you.

—Visit the sick, visit those in the Hospital, you may someday conduct their funeral.

—Start multiple Bible Studies for all age groups, but get others too lead them

—Visit the home bound

—Don't teach a Sunday School class, or a Wednesday night class, you don't have time.

—Even visit those you don't like

—Don't touch the money

—Don't get caught up in arguments like Calvinism Vs. Arminianism

—Don't do face book

—don't home school your kids, put them in a Christian school.

—Don't do stupid, never meet alone with one woman

—Baptize all you can

—Make sure the church's current financial statement is in the Sunday bulletin each week. But don't touch the money.

—Spend quality time with your Wife and Kids

—After you get there, if you discover that this is a King James only congregation, resign immediately. They won't change.

Stay in constant contact with your Director of Missions. If you are not Southern Baptist, find a mentor that you can pray with. Because you will need him. And he will be glad to see you. If you don't like visiting and praying for old sick people you are in the wrong profession. Uncle Lester taught us to pray for the sick. And He was Methodist.

Pastors, you don't need to go to seminary, and acquire student loans, because God does not call the equipped, God equips the called. If the pulpit committee chairman insists that you work on a seminary PhD degree, God forbid, you probably don't what to stay with that church. Move on.

Let me share a success story about my good friend and retired pharmacist, John Wellbaum, who never graduated from High School! When John was growing up in central Alabama during the Korean war, there was a shortage of men for the military. The Alabama National Guard allowed high school students to join the state National Guard. Which John did. Then his guard unit was called up, before he finished High School. After the war was over, he enrolled in Howard College (later renamed Samford University) under the GI bill with no High School diploma. Later he graduated from Pharmacy School at Alabama Polytechnical College (later renamed Auburn University) with a BS in Pharmacy. Still without a high school diploma and with no student loans. You too, pastor can do what John did, but the path through todays WOKE military will not be as easy John's path. If you get lucky you might exit the military as an airline pilot. Which is a marketable skill.

Finally, a Word about Church Security. It is very unlikely that your church will never experience a shooting. But if a bad guy comes to your church, be ready for him? Here is what you should do as a minimum.

1. Recruit a retired police officer to head your security team. Then train your security team through one or more of the security training classes being taught by a number of organizations. The Fellowship of Christian Peace Officers, FCPO-USA[19] has 260 chapters across the country. Find a chapter near you and ask them to train you. Then implement what they tell you. Your location is unique.

2. As a minimum they will need to lock all the outside doors to your Sanctuary except the main door on Sunday morning. At least two ushers must be stationed at the main door at all times.

3. You need someone in the parking lot greeting people as they get out of their cars. He is looking for that bad guy with a violin case. When the shooter sees your man in the parking lot, he will most likely just drive on to the next church down the road.

4. You may need a sign that says, "all backpacks and large bags are subject to search" And someone needs to be at the door to challenge anyone bringing in a large bag or rifle.

5. If your state has an open carry policy, they will need a sign that says "No Firearms allowed"

Tennessee is a permit less carry state, most citizens can open carry. There are some restrictions, learn what they are. Do the hard work.

Good Luck.

Chapter 27

Conclusion

So, what's the bottom-line Grandson? If you are really called to the ministry, there may be more than one path to success. PRAY about it. Right now, you have to make some hard decisions. But as we have stated over and over, ministry is hard work. Remember "God does not call the equipped, He equips the called" If you are young, you must first find someone willing to through you off the porch like Daffy? If you are retired, and have a comfortable retirement income, like we have and you are sure you are called to preach as we are, there is a clear path forward. You just have to find your Hill Crest Baptist Church. Your local Baptist Associations Director of Missions, DM, will help you find that church. You will need some training, but you don't need to leave home. And you sure don't need a PhD. The Samford University's Ministry Training Institute, MTI program[20] can provide all the training you need. And the training is fun. MTI is a non-degree academic program that has been equipping ministers and lay-leaders to live out their calling to serve Jesus Christ and his church for 72 years. Each course is biblically based and administered with the highest quality and integrity. The cost is only $50 for each 8-week class. The MIT program is the only program at Samford that delibly loses money each year. After you take the first class, you will be hooked. You can take each class by zoom one night a week. You never leave home. These classes are all taught by experienced local ministers. You just need internet access. But if you want the comradery of fellow pastors, you can drive out to the local Baptist association office or a local church for the 3 hours class each a week. Eventually Kevin Blackwell at

Samford or your local DM may even ask you to teach one of the classes.

But what if you are young and don't have a retirement income? First get a degree in engineering, or computer science or math, something that pays money. Then take the best Job you can find. If you don't do college, there are lots of 40 hour per week jobs out there that pay over $14 per hour. Work Hard. But don't take two jobs. You will soon burn out if try to work more than 40 hours per week. Take MTI classes until you feel comfortable enough to applying for a part time pastor opening. Find a small church, where you can grow and study the Book of Job, like I did with lots of support. Or a large church that will mentor you on the Book of Job. If you can do music, or operate a sound board, or up-date a web page, or you understand cyber security, there are many opportunities. Just remember "God does not call the equipped, He equips the called." If you truly are called, God will make a way.

One of the best ways to learn a craft, is through a Union Training program. You get paid while you learn. But it is very difficult to get into a union Training program unless you have a good friend or relative in that union. But check it out. Unions are like the communist party, if you are inside the tent you are fat and happy. But If you are outside the tent, no one cares about you, just don't get out of line. There must always be enough tough people inside the tent to keep those of us outside the tent under control. The only reason that our country needs electric cars, is so our government can just turn off a switch, and us peasants outside the tent, cannot travel. And an electrical car may catch on fire if sprayed with salt water like some did in Florida after hurricane Ian in 2022. Remember, global warming is a hoax. Never buy an electric car except maybe a golf cart. Only read your bible, your Sunday School quarterly, and *The Baptist and Reflector* (the monthly state Baptist paper in Tennessee), the *NRA Journal* and the *Epoch Times*.

When my son, Will Goins had finished his freshman year studying engineering at Tennessee Tech, he had the summer free. I suggested that he apply for a camp ranger job at the Philmont Scout Ranch in New Mexico. He had been there for a short backpacking adventure, but he was at that time not what anyone would judge to be a wilderness expert. The first thing Philmont did was send him to wilderness leadership training conducted by the National Outdoor Leadership School NOLS. This school is recognized as the best wilderness training program in the country, maybe the world. After he completed his NOLS training and trained backpacking groups all summer, anyone would easily recognize him as a wilderness expert, with all the leadership skills and self-confidence associated a true wilderness expert. At one point he even found himself standing between a pair of bear cubs and their mother. A very teachable moment. My prayer grandkids is that you too can have a learning experience like Will had at Philmont that summer.

Final thought, if you are 18, have you considered the military? They are still taking applications. My good friend Frank Conger entered the army as a private first-class PFC and finished 30 years later as a Brigadier General. The current annual salary for a brigadier general is between $145,000 and $202,000. However, the military has become very WOKE during the recent Biden administration. Understand that America is on a collision course with China and Russia. If you are in the military, you will likely see combat. And you may die. You may see that combat in a deacons meeting or in a church business meeting. The bully will show up. You will not die but you will want to. Be ready. If you are filling an interim pulpit position, we recommend you read Barbara Child and Keith Kron's book,[22] In the Interim. You may be like the emergency room Doctor, patching up the hurt in a broken church.

As we stated in Chapter 1, we have often felt like Amos writing to the nation of Israel. Our message is the same as his. God allowed Israel to be captured by Assyria, and Judah to be captured by Babylon. How long will it be before God allows America to fall to the Chinese and Russians? With the path we are currently on, it won't be long. Major changes are needed in our public education system so students will once again study the bible, learn to love God, learn to work hard and not depend on the government. Have we convinced you to never vote for a liberal? And never buy a lottery ticket. Or bet on a racehorse. Uncle Lester always owned at least two dogs.

The Epoch Times[19] has just reported that there has been a rapid increase in cancer deaths since the COVID vaccinations started. It appears that the COVID vaccines are causing cancer cells to grow faster, and more people are dying from cancer. What is absolute frightening is that the CDC manipulated the data to cover this up. We cannot trust the government.

In summary, you will need the Wisdom to know or discern which door God is opening or closing, for decisions that need to be made today. Where will this wisdom come from? If you just listen, God's Holy Spirit will guide you to always make good decisions. Don't lessen to the voices of those young men that Jeroboam lessened too. Seek out mature Godly council. Finley, did we convince you too never ever vote for a liberal? And remember pastor, when you are in the pulpit, think like a success and act like a success because you are representing the greatest success of all times. Finally, don't read anything except your bible, your Sunday school quarterly, *Judicial Watch*, *Focus on the Family*, and *The Epoch Times*. And remember never vote for a democrat.

As we were making the final revisions to this text, we learned that President Biden had signed yet another dumb exertive order. This one dumber than the open Mexican Border stupidity and the millions he has dumped at the big lie global warming. This latest dumb order deals with biotechnology and biomanufacturing. It is just a blank check for some big companies to spend lots of money. The communist's goal is to control us humans by programing us the way computers are programed. The teacher's union, has become a branch of the democrat party, is already doing this to our kids. Public schools don't emphasize spelling and math anymore. They teach critical race theory, global warming, white privilege, male privilege and the great reset theory. Critical Race Theory is replacing Marxism whose proponents want to end America as we know it. This extreme ideology is infecting our whole society. Our tax dollars are being abused and our rights attacked[20].

To understand this grandson, you must read *The Epoch Times* books entitled *How the Specter of Communism Is Ruling Our World.*[21] ISBN:978-1-63702-001-2, published by The Epoch Times.

Liberalism being taught in public schools is the cause of the disinclined to work movement. That is explained in the Epoch Times book sighted above. Actually, this is a 3-volume set with only the first 2 volumes published to date. Reed all three books. Bibles must be put back in schools. The liberals want electric cars so they can control when and where we travel. These crooks must be stopped.

We believe that there are lots of Uncle Lester stories out there. If you are willing to share your story, contact us and we may include your story in Volume II of this book. If you don't want your name listed, that's ok too. Email us at: wdgoins@epbfi.com.

Appendix 1

31 Biblical Virtues to Pray for Your Children

Taken directly from https://www.lifeaction.org

FAITH – I pray that faith will find root and grow in my children's hearts, that by faith they may gain what has been promised to them (Luke 17:5-6; Heb. 11:1-14).

A SERVANT'S HEART – God, please help my children develop a servant's heart, that they may serve wholeheartedly, as serving the Lord, not men (Eph. 6:7).

HOPE – May the God of hope grant that my children may overflow with hope by the power of the Holy Spirit (Rom. 15:13).

WILLINGNESS TO WORK – Teach my children, Lord, to value work and to work with all their heart, as working for the Lord and not for men (Col. 3:23).

PASSION FOR GOD – Lord, please instill in my children a soul that follows hard after You and clings passionately to You (Ps. 63:8).

SELF-DISCIPLINE – Father, I pray that my children may develop a disciplined and prudent life, doing what is right and just and fair (Prov. 1:3).

PRAYERFULNESS – Grant, Lord, that my children's lives may be marked by prayerfulness, that they may learn to pray in the Spirit on all occasions with all kinds of prayers (Eph. 6:18).

GRATITUDE – Help my children to live lives that are always overflowing with thankfulness and always giving thanks to God the Father for everything, in the name of our Lord Jesus Christ (Eph. 5:20; Col. 2:7).

A HEART FOR MISSIONS – Lord, please help my children develop a desire to see Your glory declared among the nations, Your marvelous deeds among the peoples (Ps. 96:3) PRAYER GUIDE www.lifeaction.org

SALVATION – Lord, let salvation spring up within my children, that they may obtain the salvation that is in Christ Jesus, with eternal glory (Is. 45:8; 2 Tim. 2:10).

GROWTH IN GRACE – I pray that my children may grow in the grace and knowledge of our Lord and Savior Jesus Christ (2 Pet. 3:18).

LOVE – Grant, Lord, that my children may learn to live a life of love, through the Spirit who dwells in them (Gal. 5:25; Eph. 5:2).

HONESTY AND INTEGRITY – May integrity and honesty be their virtue and their protection (Ps. 25:21).

SELF-CONTROL – Father, help my children to be different from the world, alert and self-controlled in all they do (1 Thess. 5:6).

LOVE FOR GOD'S WORD – May my children grow to find Your Word more precious than pure gold and sweeter than honey from the comb (Ps. 19:10).

JUSTICE – God, help my children to love justice as You do and act justly in all they do (Ps. 11:7; Mic. 6:8). MERCY – May my children always be merciful, just as their Father is merciful (Luke 6:36).

RESPECT – Father, grant that my children may show proper respect to everyone (themselves, others, those in authority) as Your Word commands (1 Pet. 2:17).

BIBLICAL SELF-ESTEEM – Help my children develop a strong self-esteem that is rooted in the realization that they are God's workmanship, created in Christ Jesus (Eph. 2:10).

FAITHFULNESS – Let love and faithfulness never leave my children but bind these twin virtues around their necks and write them on the tablet of their hearts (Prov. 3:3).

COURAGE – May my children always be strong and courageous in their character and in their actions (Deut. 31:6).

PURITY – Create in my children a pure heart, O God, and let that purity of heart be shown in their actions (Ps. 51:10).

KINDNESS – Lord, may my children always be kind to each other and to everyone else (1 Thess. 5:15).

GENEROSITY – Grant that my children may be generous and willing to share, and so lay up treasure for themselves as a firm foundation for the coming age (1 Tim. 6:18-19).

LOVE OF PEACE – Father, let my children make every effort to do what leads to peace (Rom. 14:19). JOY – May my children be filled with the joy given by the Holy Spirit (1 Thess. 1:6). PERSEVERANCE – Lord, teach my children perseverance in all they do, and help them especially to run with perseverance the race marked out for them (Heb. 12:1).

HUMILITY – God, please cultivate in my children the ability to show true humility toward everyone (Tit. 3:2).

COMPASSION – Lord, please clothe my children with the virtue of compassion (Col. 3:12).

RESPONSIBILITY – Grant that my children may learn responsibility, being willing to carry his own load (Gal. 6:5).

CONTENTMENT – Father, teach my children the secret of being content in any and every situation, through Your strength (Phil. 4:12-13).

ENDNOTES

[1] *The Epoch Times* Aug 3-9, 2022.

[2] *Trail to Oklahoma.*

[3] *The Manufacturing Institute*, 2020.

[4] *The Epic Times* Oct 2022.

[5] *How the Specter of Communism Is Ruling Our World,* Three Volume series, Published by The Epoch Times, New York 2022, ISBN 978-1-947150-10-2.

[6] The Epoch Times, Oct 12-18, 2022.

[7] "How the Specter of Communism is Ruling the World" published by The Epic Times ISBN 9-781947-150102.

[8] Fred Singer *Hot Talk, Cold Science,* third edition, available from Amazon.

[9] *Hot Talk, Cold Science: Global Warming's Unfinished Debate.* Third Edition by S. Fred Singer ISBN 13:978=1598133417, ISBN-10: 1598133411

[10] Allan Stein, "There is No Climate Emergency" *The Epoch Times.*

[11] https://thewartburgwatch.com

[12] Kevin Hardy and Alex Green, *Chattanooga Times Free Press,* March 3rd, 2015.

[13] John Roseman, *The Bible Parenting Code*, 2021, Carpenter's Son Publishing, 2021, ISBN 978-1-952025-69-3

[14] *Focus on the Family,* https://www.focusonthefamely.com.

[15] *Thirty-One Biblical Virtues to pray for your Child*, https://lifeaction.org.

[16] Howard Forshee "Now You Are a Deacon" can be ordered from http://lifeway.com for $11.24 plus shipping.

[17] Kent evans@manhoodjourney.org.

[18]https://christianindex.org/stories/the-four-most-common-acts-of-stupidity-that-get-pastors-fired,1829

[19] https://fcpo.org.

[20] https://www.samford.edu.

[21]. *The Narrated Bible, In Chronological Order*, F. LaGuard Smith, 1984.

[22] *In the Interim*, Barbara Child and Keith Kron, ISBN 978-1-55896-702-1.

[19] *The Epoch Times* Oct 15, 2022.

[20] *Critical Race Theory: A Citizen's Handbook*, containing all the Information and Tools You Need to Expose and Stand Up to CRT. Published by Judicial Watch, June 10, 2022. 425 third Street, Suite 800, Washington, DC 20024.

[21] *How the Specter of Communism Is Ruling Our World*. ISBN:978-1-63702-001-2, published by *The Epoch Times*, 229 W 28th Street, 7th floor, New York, NY 10001.

Final Thought

Dear Reader,

If you have read this far, you probably have an "Uncle Lester" story. If you do and you are willing to share your story, mail it to us at:

1783 Iron Works Pike
Lexington, KY 40511-8431

We will include your story in Volume 2 of *What we Learned from Uncle Lester.*

See you down the trail.